Praise for James P. Lenfestey's *A Marriage Book*

"These tender, sly, plainspoken poems are a profound (and sexy) hymn to a long marriage. Lenfestey writes of domestic matters, yes, but the poems are most definitely undomesticated. They tell a thousand small secrets in an extended meditation on love and all its consequences. They also chart the history of a complex emotion over many years, which I found fascinating. Tonally nuanced, fresh and far-ranging, the voice in these poems is a delight." —CHASE TWICHELL

"In this age of cynicism, or at the very least irony, it is good to come upon a book that celebrates marriage and family without either sentimentality or ambivalence. 'So much poetry is about storms, / bruised fruit, locusts eating everything,' Lenfestey writes. 'This poem is about a harvest that satisfies.'" —LINDA PASTAN

"Warning Label: prepare to be shaken, moved, amused, terrified, relieved, delighted. Take in small doses or one large gulp; either way, you will be healed. These poems are alive with many things: stories, images, metaphors, but more than anything else they are alive with rhythm. These are poems of mutual passion, but also of heartbreak and solitude. In the final stanza of 'My Wife Sleeping as I Drive,' Lenfestey writes: 'We plunge along our course of earth, / each alert in our own way, / ahead the blue-black sky full / of oncoming lights and stars.' How amazing that we have been invited along for the ride!" —JIM MOORE

"Think of Lenfestey's *A Marriage Book* as a talking photo album or an unfolding epithalamium. The lovers meet and marry; the children arrive and grow up. Along the way, there are days of joy and anxious nights, sweetness and humor. The narrator is a courageous 'captain,' an 'old shepherd / exhausted with tending,' and a 'Marco Polo,' but like his pre͟ ͟ ͟ ͟ ͟ ͟ ͟ ͟ he always returns to his center, his wife, who is (as ͟ ͟ ͟ ͟ ͟ ͟ ͟ ͟ tribute to fifty years of real-world l͟ ͟ ͟ ͟

"Lenfestey's poems encircle a marriage while opening it out into the depths and heights with tenderness—I might say reverence—and grace. The poems move from outer rituals into the interior world of the self that wants to make sense of birth, joy, damage, death, and grief, but can't, entirely. You want to know how it is to stay through the long haul? Look to these poems. 'It is gravity, / which limits us totally, / which makes all life possible,' Lenfestey writes. These are the poems of a brave heart and a skilled poet. They will make you want to kiss your sweetheart." —FLEDA BROWN

"I've been an avid reader of Lenfestey's work for many years. His *Seeking the Cave* was a wonder, and so is his *Marriage Book*, a collection rooted in passion, desire, sensuality, and the 'shared heat' of love. This is, above all, a book of transcendence, of celebration. Containing a wealth of extraordinary poems, it appears to have been conceived in a beautiful sustained burst of illumination, with Lenfestey overlapping his themes to create a collection so seamless it could well be read as one long poem. This is a truly superb book, an absolute joy to read." —ROBERT HEDIN

"I just finished reading *A Marriage Book* straight through. Such a treasure. Virtuosic, with all the different moods and colors and shadings and statements and counterstatements, and so beautiful. A very wonderful book." —ELIZABETH GORDON MCKIM

"These generous poems, attractive in their emotional directness, confident in their subject matter, bring us into contact with the intimacies of an intensely lived life, insisting both on their frequent joys—there is playfulness, there is fervor—and on disclosing the vulnerabilities that demanding relationships reveal in us over the decades." —MICHAEL DENNIS BROWNE

A MARRIAGE

BOOK: 50 YEARS

of POEMS *from*

A MARRIAGE

ALSO BY JAMES P. LENFESTEY

POETRY

Earth in Anger: Twenty-Five Poems of Love and Despair for Planet Earth

A Cartload of Scrolls: One Hundred Poems in the Manner of T'ang Dynasty Poet Han-Shan

Into the Goodhue County Jail: Poems to Free Prisoners

The Toothed and Clever World

Saying Grace

Odalisque

Low Down and Coming On: A Feast of Delicious and Dangerous Poems about Pigs (editor)

If Bees Are Few: A Hive of Bee Poems (editor)

NONFICTION

The Urban Coyote: Howlings on Family, Community and the Search for Peace and Quiet

Robert Bly in This World (coeditor)

Seeking the Cave: A Pilgrimage to Cold Mountain

A MARRIAGE

BOOK: 50 YEARS

of POEMS *from*

A MARRIAGE

JAMES P. LENFESTEY

MILKWEED EDITIONS

Published 2017 by Milkweed Editions
Printed in the United States of America
Cover design by Mary Austin Speaker
Author photo by Larry Marcus
18 19 20 21 5 4 3 2
First Edition

Milkweed Editions, an independent nonprofit publisher, gratefully acknowl-
edges sustaining support from the Jerome Foundation; the Lindquist &
Vennum Foundation; the McKnight Foundation; the National Endowment
for the Arts; the Target Foundation; and other generous contributions from
foundations, corporations, and individuals. Also, this activity is made possible
by the voters of Minnesota through a Minnesota State Arts Board Operating
Support grant, thanks to a legislative appropriation from the arts and cultural
heritage fund, and a grant from Wells Fargo. For a full listing of Milkweed
Editions supporters, please visit milkweed.org.

Library of Congress Cataloging-in-Publication Data

Names: Lenfestey, James P., author.
Title: A marriage book / James P. Lenfestey.
Description: First edition. | Minneapolis, Minnesota : Milkweed
Editions,
    2017.
Identifiers: LCCN 2017039309 | ISBN 9781571314925 (pbk. : alk.
paper)
Subjects: LCSH: Marriage--Poetry.
Classification: LCC PS3612.E528 A6 2017 | DDC 811/.6--dc23
LC record available at https://lccn.loc.gov/2017039309

Milkweed Editions is committed to ecological stewardship. We strive to align
our book production practices with this principle, and to reduce the impact of
our operations in the environment. We are a member of the Green Press
Initiative, a nonprofit coalition of publishers, manufacturers, and authors
working to protect the world's endangered forests and conserve natural
resources. *A Marriage Book* was printed on acid-free 100% postconsumer-
waste paper by Thomson-Shore.

for Susan

Contents

In the final analysis, poets and novelists will have more to say about love than psychologists, for they express the inexpressible, and describe individual persons and their love problems, with their individual solutions and failures, and this is true to life and to eros.

John Sanford, *The Invisible Partners*

PROLOGUE

WHO WOULD BELIEVE

Even a good poet must be wary as a spider
offering a book of love poems
to the woman he married fifty years ago.
If he exaggerates his love, she'll know.
If he denies it, she'll devour him
while remembering her old dead lovers.
If he sands off the edge of his desire,
what's the point?
And if his desire for her is undiminished,
who would believe?

PART ONE

Lie Love Easy

LIE LOVE EASY

pores, pouring, pouring over
lying under, lying, lie
stroke soft furry truths
in the lap
pet soft purring truths
in the lap
take a long time
jiggle hills easy
love time
gentle hills roll

lick your fur
lick your fur, cat
make a breeze
in the forest tangle
kiss the slick
leaves
one and one
become easy
ease away
the forest anger
lie love
please, no dread
please, no leaving
lie love easy

AERIE AND HIGH

I call to her from across
the room,
she hears hawks
high over rolling hills

we arc up, roll and join
and roll away,
high eyes glistening down

I brush her once here,
graze her once there,
she feels wings

I give her my licks of wing,
sharp flicks of talon,
my rough, cruel voice,
my down

we fall
we fall

we fall
toward that river
that soil
that call

Aerie and high

aerie and deep
we nest there
we nest there
    and sleep.

SHARED HEAT

There is a certain hairy roughness
to overcome, I understand,
for me it is all easy,
like biting into warm
sour cream.

To touch, then
near sleep,
to fold together
like egg whites, like gears,
then sleep without touching,
sharing heat.

Shared heat.
Is this not the peace and comfort
of the species?
Why we gather under heavy
robes in winter?
Why we sew together
such huge quilts?

Roll apart, not touching
in the night sleep.
But never far,
never too far,
from the heat.

WOODSMOKE AND PERFUME

As a boy, there were
few women.

There was the woman
who smelled of woodsmoke
and the woman
who smelled of perfume.

There was the woman to be
danced with
for the last dance,
and the woman to walk home
holding her hand.

The woman who
wanted to be loved
and lay there,
and the

woman who wanted to love
and I lay there.

And the woman who said no
while our minds went mad,
and the woman who said yes
who went mad.

And the woman who said no
who called and said yes
and the woman who went mad
who never called.

And then the woman
who said yes
and yes and again yes,
you asshole, not that way.

Yes.

TO MAKE A BABY

These days it takes courage.

No one has enough money.
Nobody has enough time.
No way is there enough room
in the house.

So you find yourself crowded
into that double bed.
And the kids are asleep.
The checkbook's downstairs.
You bump into something warm.

And you find your courage rising.

AN ENGINEERING PROBLEM

What would you do?

I was asleep.
She tried to entice me.
She arched herself over me
like a pre-tensioned bridge beam.
The smooth arc of her calves
was enough to drive retired engineers
to recalculate fundamental forces—
the tensile strength of skin,
the compressive strength of thighs,
the pressure and flow dynamics of laying
mile after mile of pipe
underground.

Where do you get off? I inquired.
In the bathtub, she responded.
She asked me to join her.

But this groggy engineer
couldn't do the calculations:
displacement, volume,
there's no room for two
is all I could figure.
Don't worry, she said,
we'll work it out.

What would you do?

Here's what I did.

I got up.
I wrote a poem.

While she soaked and softened,
I typed uncalculated lines
in my office next to the bathtub.

I could hear the water rustle
once, twice, a hundred times.

She entered my office from behind me
as I typed.

She wore a nightgown with pores of lace,
hair piled loosely, ringlets dipped
in water touching her neck.
She was warm and soft and groggy
as she hung her heavy arms around me.
"I love your poems," she said.

We built a bridge.

THE BATH

I caught her as she slipped
into the tub.
She held him in her hands,
flushed and embarrassed.

Then settled
into the tendrils of steam
curling off the surface,
eyes heavy with his heft.

She ran her slick fingers up
and down his spine.
He's deep, she said.
And endlessly fascinating.
And I love him, I love him.

My eyes burned through the water
toward the tangled story I call home.
But his chapters are long, she said.
And he's such a fine . . . writer.

I stumbled to our bed, determined
to take matters into my own hands.
I reached for García Márquez
and was soon lost in tangled limbs
and the seduction of rivers.

I rolled and moaned
while her tub stayed hot
as pages turned
faster and faster.

AFTER SHE SLEEPS

After she sleeps
no end of possibilities . . .

Mixtures of chocolate chip
ice cream, bananas
and pears.

Drinking amber maple syrup
direct from the can.

Ecstatic readings of Kabir
and Cold Mountain
with much strutting
and waving of arms
before the refrigerator.

A story composed for the children
on the cold marble table
about riding winged snails
on their slime trails
into perilous encounters.

And how bears, when together,
tend to mumble
which is why bears are so big.

And ketchup on fresh poetry,

mushrooms sautéed with wordplay,
a plateful on the side
next to sweet ice cream
and burnt morning coffee.

She knows all about it
and it's all right.
Just leave the kitchen clean
in the morning.

LUNCH-MAKING

Crumbs cast enormous shadows
under the track lights
onto the marble table—

cracker bits from the baby,
sugar crystals, coffee grounds,
a towering Cheerio,
fallen stamens under the plant.

I did not see any of these before.
To me they belonged in the kitchen
with the silverware, the stove,
the other household gods.

The goddess sees otherwise.
She refuses to reign in this place
unless there are neither crumbs
nor the shadows of crumbs.

I have slowly seen the light
glancing off freshly wiped marble.
To her it is very satisfactory.
Now lunch-making can begin.

SATURDAY NIGHT

Small doses
on Saturday night
of a fine meal and
good theatre and
afterward a chocolate torte
with crème fraîche and
cappuccino and then Irish coffee
and when you get home
the kids are asleep and
the babysitter's paid
and a bolt on the door
and a few whiffs of the vapors
and magically
in the act of touching her
a small series of explosions
under the fingertips
and fantasies become realities
in prolonged processions
and wife
rhymes with life.

OH GOD, HOW DEEP

Spring orchards leave me weak
in blazing petals, my
nose covered with pollen.

Most wait to eat the fruit. I can't,
buzzing to the vibrance
of white blossoms, sweetness
somewhere deep within.

At night, familiar incense rises
from her branches,
pulls me toward her like a falcon
toward a sparrow,
like mist above cool water.

Yes, whispers the soft stem
of my spine.
Yes, I will do anything.
Oh God, how deep.

THEY WILL HAVE TO UNDERSTAND

The sales managers line up
before breakfast
for their ad campaigns
and the CEO chews on me
for lunch
and the Annual Report caws
its insistent midnight deadline in my ear
and when I rub my eyes
I see only a red, crumbling wave.

So if I run harder into the night,
my lungs will have to understand.
If I push my dinner
into the garbage disposal
and my fork slips
and the silver spits back
mangled
and I kick the sink
and scream at the windows
and terrify the children
and my wife steps out the door
holding herself,
they will have to understand.

I do not do it often.
They will have to understand.

HERE, TAKE THIS POEM

I am explaining my side of the story
in a courtroom.
Each dish done, oil changed, fire built
is notched in my belt.
Each key forgotten, garage door stuck,
toilet paper roll unmounted
is billed against her.

On and on, evening the record
against her relentless prosecution:
underwear on the floor, hair
in the sink, late again for dinner.

For a decade I have tried this case.
Judgment radiates off me like darts.
But the courtroom is secret:
no cameras, no reporters,
nothing spoken out loud, ever.

Today, the case is close to resolution.
Today I will tell her.
Here, take this poem.

EVEN AS THE PASSION COOLS

Were you to construct a temple
of thighs,
a Grand Canyon of thighs,
a kachina of the thigh spirits,
a wooden bowl of white fermented milk,
a chalice of wine . . .

Were I to construct a cross,
my forearm softly across your throat,
your menorah of wide-stretched limbs,
the drumbeats of supplicant societies
pulsing inside you,
and dancers,
hundreds of them,
and hoards of dreamy reptiles . . .

The temple of the Lord
is a deep canyon,
the church a riverbed,
the bed the reflected river clouds,
the coverlet the movement of sand grains,
the song a flute of reeds,
the bank the riverbank,
the deposit
a pool of silver minnows,
the book the geology
of pink walls,

the astronomy a slit
of black stars overhead.

A coyote howls in the canyon.
Marmots look up from their
stiff grazing.
Fish stop swimming and are carried
downstream by the current.
And particular white moths flutter down
in clouds
over the extended white fingers
of a plant of spines.

When they touch, new gods are born,
even as the passion cools.

THE HAND OF GOD

... nothing can be sole or whole
that has not been rent.

—W. B. YEATS

Blue is the color of my true love's veins.
Red her cracked and bleeding lips.
Salt tides cascade through her hair.
Hurricanes hiss at teeth and cheeks.

As the ocean inside her rolls,
as she makes room.

As she makes room,
flowering herself,
petal by petal.
As she makes room,
standing on herself,
step by step.

Push, urges the doctor.
Push, pleads the husband.
Push, demands the shocked
and dangling fish.

She hears only
the tympanum of her skin,
the melting of her bones.

Then on her face
the hand of God appears,
blue as the sea.

It flows over her stretched lips
and standing veins,
dividing her with a touch
into two slick suckling dolphins
soft as jellyfish

amid leaping saltwater cries beside her:
I believe
I believe
I believe

PART TWO

She Who Thinks Like a Fish Thinks

SELF-PORTRAIT: NEWBORN FATHER AND SON

Can a woman forget her nursing child . . . ?

—ISAIAH 49:15

Look at him,
maniac sweating in
his straightjacket,
a scalded prune,
ancient projectile,
unused warhead,
sneaky prototype!

But the cry's the thing,
air raid siren terrorizing
the night while mother
snatches bandages
of sleep between
bombing runs.

Although he can't see,
he searches, sonar honing
straight for mother's milk.
What immense, unfunny joke
was played on man, born
breastless! Worse, a paltry
mockery of the need!

Humorless, his siren wails,
bombs fall, as stunned father
and son pace back and forth
in the trembling shelter of
their upended world.

SHE WHO THINKS LIKE A FISH THINKS

for Dora at three weeks

At two in the morning, in the lake
of my wife's breathing, with headlights
floating across the ceiling,
your dark, underwater eyes sweep
toward my face. Your fingers reach,
then pull away.

You cannot place me yet
in your old aquarium cracked
and spilled to noise and light
three weeks ago tonight.

I offer you my little finger,
familiar, perhaps, as a passing eel,
and moist breath for your cheeks
so red and angry at the roughness
of our air.

But a father's breath
cannot yet calm
you who think
like a fish thinks.
Your dark eyes
and minnow fingers
swim away.

LEARNING TO SPEAK MAX

hát is anything that can fit
   on the head and be celebrated

burb, everything that flies through the air

báybee is all people

úrt is every pain

árk is without light

máma is she who pushed you out
   and pulled you back

  and

dáda, ah . . . he's the one
     who holds you
        terrified.

IF WE WERE BEARS

Belches like bear grunts
rumble from me
as I lumber along the floor
swabbing up midnight puke.

Whimpering son,
pale as moonlight,
eyes of melting ice,
breath of fiery volcanoes,

sweet sick boy, try to sleep.
Let our mammalian memories
erase the scent
of all this wasted food.

If we were bears,
we could sleep inside the earth
until we're well again. As
humans, we can only hibernate

in each other's arms till nausea,
that red-hatted hunter,
gives up and quietly
goes home.

SINGING THE BABIES TO SLEEP

Crib in the closet, another up
the stairs with the rope rail,
every night home I sing the babies to sleep—

Irene good night, Irene good night,
with Huddie Ledbetter, Pete Seeger,
my father, mother, cousins, and
sisters singing *Irene* together by heart.

I stroke them with my hands
up and down unsettled backs as I sing
(they slept on their tummies then), bathed and
snugged by Susan into cotton sacks.

Stop your rambling, stop your gambling,
Stop staying out late at night,
Go home to your wife and family,
Stay there by the fireside bright.

I sing until we all sleep, they in their cribs,
and the man bent over them, exhausted from
staying up late at night, the rambling, the
gambling, home now by the fireside bright.

DON'T LEAVE ALBERT EINSTEIN WITH THE KIDS!

Don't leave Albert Einstein
with the kids!
He'll abandon them behind the
cabbage at the supermarket
while calculating love
at the speed of squeeze.

He'll lose them in the park
watching love bend like light
round the swing set, astonished
at the grip of its gravity.

He finds love more strange,
charmed, up, down,
top, bottom,
than ever known
before a child's birth—
a fundamental force.

MONSTER AT THE BREAKFAST TABLE

He stomps downstairs,
FE FI FO FUM, demanding
breakfast blood and bones.

Eyes hooded by tangled hair
flare if whims
aren't promptly served
by morning slaves.

But this round table holds
neither knights nor knaves,
only more monsters
tangled in their own loose
shirts and untied shoes
as the school bus dragon rumbles
and belches its hideous black
and yellow armor
toward our gate.

When it eats these grisly morsels
for the day,
the king and queen lean low
and clink our morning mead.

WHEN YOU ARE READY, CLIMB

You hug your mother like a life vest,
shun me like deep water.

I know. She saved your life.
At the instant of your birth
she knew you were too blue.
She woke the doctor, me,
you both so frightened then
you cling to each other now
as if there were no gravity.

I wait.
When you are ready,
climb.
Pull my branches.
Crack my limbs.
Strip my leaves.

My roots are deep.
As deep as I am tall.
As wide as I am deep.

When you are ready,
climb.

STRAWBERRIES

With my children
I more eager than they
through the rows
stooping with joy

Racing back to the car
far too many sweet quarts
berries falling like
red pebbles
on the green path

ANGEL AT EIGHTH-GRADE GRADUATION

Two plus parrot plus
egg plus wing plus sky.
How much is it worth, Max?
I know you know.

You were born with
the feathers of archangels.

When your bicycle crashed
into the streetlight
your broken wheel sang
like a harp.

When your skateboard soared
into a stop sign,
your forearm snapped
in a puff of quills.

Nothing in school can ground
that flight.
But teachers will help
improve your landings.
So when you do touch down,
nothing truly valuable
will be broken.

And your life, a flock
of untamed birds, will somehow
turn away from danger
en masse, as if at signal.

IF YOU BECOME A MONK

To children, earth is flat as a yard,
labor the distance a lawn mower cuts.
Food is fast. Bed is home.

Only with decades of study will
you discover more substantial fare.
So when you find yourself
driving a tractor back and forth
beneath the iron lid of the horizon,
or driving an iron across damp sheets,
or shifting papers against the iron
ticking of the office clock,
you will have a chest of treasure
to open in your mind.

And if you become a monk,
what wonders will occupy your cell!

TO A YOUNG DAUGHTER

For then I scorn to change my state with kings.

—SHAKESPEARE, SONNET 29

It is not the icing laid
in lines over the wild cherries.
Nor the cube of crystals
next to the bitter coffee.
Nor the cap of whipped cream
sheltering the hot chocolate.

It is your smile, sly at the eye,
corner perked in self-love,
that whirls me in sweetness,
that lays me in an orchard
in full bloom.

TO MY DAUGHTER AT FOURTEEN IN THE AFTERMATH OF THE FIRST FULL MOON

Men will never understand you.
You are too deep for them,
too rich.

They will stand in front of you
for hours
with nothing to say.

Then they will say it,
and it will be nothing.

Understand that males, for all their power
and all their mind and all their wit,
are awash in awe.
It laps at their ankles
like waves breaking on a beach.

Yes, you can count on them to protect you
when bats wake you in the night
and you scream and scream and scream.
But it is best to count on yourself,
even in the matter of bats.

Hitting them with a broom
and carrying them out to the garden
with their broken wings and stunned,

high-pitched bleating,
is a nasty business.
But somebody has to do it.
Don't let him be the only one to learn
that the bat that fills the echoing halls
of your nightmares
barely fills the palm of your hand.
Like a hummingbird, it is practically weightless.

Now that you are a woman, you can learn the truth:
nobody likes to kill bats.

And men, huge and blue-eyed sailors in your dreams,
are practically weightless in the palm of your hand.

DRIVING LESSON: TO MY SON AT SIXTEEN

Driving a car is the least of your worries.
It can kill you in an instant.
A woman can wreck you
in the rearview mirror.

Women are like pianos.
In the beginning you hit the wrong keys
and nobody likes it.
Sometimes the key cover
slams down on your knuckles.
Sometimes not.

To be good,
you have to learn how to play:
allegro, andante, vivace, moderato,
misterioso, grosso, profondo.

Yet some days
they remain out of tune
regardless of your persistence,
your practice.

Your timing is bad.

Forget harmony.
Go play the violin.
Go drive the car.

CHORES

Chores every day, no debate.
Table set, dishes washed, garbage out.
No car keys without gas money.
No gas money without grass cut.

And then at sixteen she
drives off one Saturday night
and doesn't come home.
And the policewoman's bored reassurance
at 4 a.m. does not reassure at all.

And when she drives up the street
a few minutes past noon the next day
it takes a decade of hard work
to figure out who we all are now.

ACRES OF DIAMONDS

> *Hush, little baby, don't say a word.*
> *Daddy's gonna buy you a mockingbird.*
> *And if that mockingbird don't sing,*
> *Daddy's gonna buy you a diamond ring.*

An overdose?
An overdose of what?
Of diamond rings?
Of glass?

A looking glass.
A cart rolled over.
No more pretty baby.
Didn't the mockingbird sing
for you, my daughter?

I stand before the looking glass,
no more pretty baby in my arms
reaching for my worn finger.
Now you grip the steering wheel
to change freeway lanes.
We thought that would add chance
and terror enough.

But you felt stuck, you said,
stuck with the Plains warriors:
Is it real?

Is it real,
this life I am living?
And no way to test it,
to prove it.

Didn't the mockingbird sing for you,
my darling daughter?
There were acres of diamonds
at home.
They were all
for you.

PRAYER

I left my daughter alone
like a sheep
left alone
with a pacing moon.

I walked the mile to my hotel
from her college room
with barbed wire stretched
through my back.

I lay in my bed,
an old shepherd
exhausted with tending,
stomach sick with the taste
of bad water.

Even through thick walls
I could hear the howling
deep inside her head,
see her shy reflection
in the water.

She huddled alone in moon shadow
against the stares of her own eyes,
pitiless and knife-toothed.

I did what I could—
cobbled a rough shelter
out of windfall,
lit a hazy lamp,
gave blood,
tucked covers.
I was limping myself,
silent as an empty bell.

In the moonlight through the window
I see my gray beard rise and fall,
rise and fall
with ancient syllables
laying me down to sleep,
I pray the Lord my soul to keep.
If she should die before I wake
I pray the Lord my soul to take.

amen
amen
amen

FOR A RESCUED DAUGHTER, AN ARTIST, COMING UP FOR AIR THROUGH WATER

Everyone knows where the waterline is.
Below feels like home,
but humans die there. Drowned,
it is called. And dead it is.
But soft, floating death, like living fish,
or flowing muslin folds, or sleep long longed-for.

Water mitigates gravity,
eliminates needs like bathrooms
and beds and cooking and cleaning
and loving and hating.

Above the waterline lies rough air,
one rasping breath after another, wind,
steep hills, and thin, gasping mountains.

Yet you breathe on,
for your husband, sons, and
one taut canvas after another.

Like a phase change:
Watery blood and skin and hair
transmuted to watery blue-green paint,
watery paint becoming shadows
and the shadows of shadows.

Amid the daily clamor of puffing
swimmers and climbers,
a divine talent, ascending.

BACKSCRATCH BOY

Your righteousness
is mighty as a king's.
Your anger lasts the time
an egg cooks.
Your smile charms cobras
and cataracts.
Your indolence is a jungle
in which butterflies live whole lives.

But we can scratch each other's
backs for hours,
like monkeys quiet in the trees
or baboons squatting
in the grass.
Your hands salve
old wounds in my back,
while I find in yours a billion
nerve endings that all shriek joy.

A WILD WOOD

This rangy son across restaurant
eggs and toast is twenty-one.
He breaks me up as jokes
slip from his tongue like crumbs.
And when he hugs, his arms float
wide as wings, an unobstructed
heart wide open chest to chest.

But I hear the rumble in his gut.
His eyes sweep the floor like brooms
with dreams and fears.

Outside this sidewalked town
and college by a lake
lies a wild wood. Inside live
hairy hogs that bite and
won't let go.

It is time for him
to feel those teeth
that drag you to the ground,
against which you must
battle for your life.

TROUBADOUR SONG

It happened the way the troubadours
said it would—through the eyes.

His arm emerged from the window
of a small plane. She remembers
the sun-illuminated hairs, the woven veins.

Later, he saw her across a room.
He could not look again, nor speak.

Now she marks her textbooks
with his photograph,
reading in the company of his eyes.

Touch too has come, and strategy.
He conspires to escape to visit her,
a thousand miles for a single day.
She asserts her need to study.

But the eyes have opened
the windows of two souls,
across a runway,
a table, a room, half a continent.

Children will have those eyes.

MORNING OF THE WEDDING

On our early morning walk, the dog,
unwell, eats grass.
A tug labors a barge toward a splash
of sunlight on the lake.
Four cormorants fly by my shoulder.
Gulls carry on their obnoxious calling.

August 22, 1992. August?
No more than any other month.
Yet in the peace of early morning light
among the ripe raspberries of this
particular late summer season,
with the clap of horses rising the hill,
the world is changed forever
by these two courageous children.

Kneeling and touching an old gold ring
and making it burst into flame before us
with a few quiet syllables
from their bursting hearts,
mathematics and grammar implode.
Two become one,
I do becomes we are,
and infinity, that shimmering abstraction,
twists into a particular
double helix.

The splash
of sunlight on the lake
winks at me three times,
and smiles.

MIDNIGHT CALL

A friend took his from a silent skid on ice,
his daughter's brain waves a straight line.
Another heard his message on the news.

Tonight a distant moan rings our sleep.
Our son, neck broken, climbed for help,
his wife wrapped in the car's crushed cab.

At his birth we learned to listen
with our spines for broken
sounds like these.
On his wedding day we felt
her bones knit with our own.

Tonight, car lights race across the ceiling,
each one a phone, each phone ringing.
Without complaint, we answer.
We answer. We answer.

CHRISTMAS PRAYER, SANTA FE, DECEMBER 25, 1993

The ER nurse glances up.
Is my son sleeping?
Yes. And his wife?
Yes, she is sleeping.
You should too.

Outside, dawn stretches its golden arm
through a saddle in black mountains,
Sangre de Cristo, blood of Christ,
rounded, strangely female.

I walk and walk in the cold.
A grove of juniper and piñon
opens before me, a roadside chapel.
I pray.

I praise the east for the sun,
rising again in our lives.
And the trees of the eastern mountains
for their strength to hold the tumbling car
in their arms. I thank the trees.

I praise the west for the Jemez Mountains,
born of fiery calamity, and the village
riding her sturdy shoulders
a thousand years.

I praise the north, St. Vincent's hospital,
its sharp, clean edges outlined in light
against soft mountains.

I praise the south, for the road that brought me
here, praise the builders of roads,
and the snowplow drivers who worked
all night that I might safely arrive.

I praise my grandfather below, who practiced
surgery on vagrant children in Vienna that my son's
wife may walk again today.
Praise his strong jaw, his pipe, the sharp
scalpel in his warm hands.

I praise the bowl of sky
filled with clouds of living breath
from my lungs and theirs,
the same moist smoke since life began.

Are they sleeping?
Yes.
Will they recover?
That is up to gods
like these.

ON A YOUNGEST DAUGHTER'S ACCEPTANCE
AT THE COLLEGE OF HER CHOICE

A red door opens toward a cornfield.
Rows of stalks bear heavy golden heads.
Cribs and bins wait empty to be filled.

God made the weather and blue-green water.
Parents work night and day
to bring home every golden child.

So much poetry is about storms,
bruised fruit, locusts eating everything.
This poem is about a harvest that satisfies.

ON COURSE

At dawn, our youngest daughter
rises for her summer job.
Now I'm the intruder as she races
through morning rites, bed made,
dishes to the sink, newspaper splayed.

In a month she'll live away at school
and for the first time in three decades
the pressure inside this house will equalize
with the shade under outside elms.

After the door slams, sudden stillness.
Ice tumbles to the freezer tray like calving glaciers.
A cardinal whistles through two panes of glass.

I listen, steady, like a captain at the helm,
white beard signaling the wisdom of the course,
storms abating, grandchildren reaching
for my knees, my logbooks.

ONCE IN THE SIXTIES

after William Stafford

When she walked toward me
radiant with pregnancy,
we laughed as if shaken
by some unseen wind
propelling our van
those long camping miles.

Children grew like wildflowers,
so obvious, green and yellow,
quick out of the ground.

We remember their firelit
faces from old photographs,
their unexpected humors congealing
around the campfire.

We barely had time to wonder at their beauty,
grades, spouses, children
and we are camping again,
under dark pines,
near lapping water.

PART THREE

And Still She Blooms

IN HER GARDEN, SHE

I am thinking she
does not know how to be happy.
Looking up over my book, I
expect familiar clouded brows,
earth heavy on her shoulders,
family boulders in her pockets.

Then she rises from her garden.
I see sunflowers bow toward her hair,
pea blossoms steal up her thigh,
sky blue forget-me-nots simulate her eyes.
As she stoops again to dig,
clumps of roses,
brilliant all season,
reach low to brush her glove.

My eyes visit her like hungry butterflies.
We feed, grateful, as if such
beauty could just happen here,
so quiet, in front of our house.

TWO KNIVES

She spends whole days cutting
vegetables, I cutting meat.

We argue over the proper gift
to give a friend for his wedding:
I want serrated,
she wants sharp and smooth.

The same week she trimmed
her fingertip into the celery,
I wrote two poems:
one of love, one of war,
serrated and sharp at once.

Oh how the hot blood flowed!

FALL COLORS

That maple, burning yellow,
balds from the top.
Nearby elms drop shriveled husks
revealing graceful dancer's arms.
The euonymus becomes a ball of rose.
Buckthorns stubbornly stay green.

So you and I can be different too.
You hang on tight to your red passion
while I let my green fall,
eager to start the next life.

DEPARTURE

Sheathed in black,
she sharpens herself
against the baggage counter,
the blade of her
straight and quick.

Be careful, she said,
this is a fragile moment
in our thirty years. Then
stepped toward United
as if a plane herself.

She flew east toward a grief so deep
it took her thirty years to name it.
I drove twelve hundred miles west
to red and angry canyons hidden
in the lies of old priests and professors.

We moved over the same earth
past our time together
toward something powerful, dark,
able to be dug up
only when alone.

EXPEDITION ALONE

In Peru the beautiful airline attendant
waved her painted fingernails in front of me.

In Peru the high school girls sat with me
as I drank cappuccino
and we practiced English for hours.

In Peru the schoolteacher's wife asked
if I wanted to buy
her butterfly collection.

In Peru the Quechua woman hurled her sack
of potatoes over the side of the truck
and pulled herself in
on top of me.

In Peru the young Catholic girl
in her gray schoolgirl's uniform
came up to my raft
parked in the sun on the riverbank.
Her teeth were as white
as the glaciers overhead,
and she gave to me from beneath
her sweater
bright oranges.

In Peru four young girls threshed corn
in the dooryard.

In Peru a woman with leather feet
cut open white chocolate beans
in the sun.

In Peru the rainy season washed out
the mountain road
and one could go no further
though roosters strolled the gap
like satyrs.

SKIN LIKE BOTTICELLI'S VENUS

How dare you be so smooth,
stranger on the mountain path?

How dare you brush
one silk thigh with the other
like wildflowers in light breeze,
the fragrance of California
sage rising around you?

Your skin sheathes you
like a fine wine's finish
sparkles along the tongue,
like memories of starlight
spilling over bent grass.

None of you I dare touch,
as I dare not touch
Botticelli's Venus's hand.

Lest I enter that
luminescent world,
grow luminous myself,
unreal, totally lost.

MY WIFE SLEEPING AS I DRIVE

She trusts no one. Even sleeping
she keeps one foot on the dashboard,
a last defense against troubles.

Without her on watch, the sleeping world
could lose its way, stumble as we
once did into old and painful traps.

At sunset, the undersides of clouds
ripple with rose and gold.
Her head heavy on her chest,
rare silhouette,
hushes me at the wheel.

Next to the highway, deer
graze corn stubble in twilight.
At their hooves, wild
turkeys look and feed.

We plunge along our course of earth,
each alert in our own way,
ahead the blue-black sky full
of oncoming lights and stars.

AND STILL SHE BLOOMS

Rains flood western mountains.
Lightning shatters eastern shores.
Ice cracks limbs, gophers siphon roots.
And still she blooms, waving
smartly over the tall grass.

Bumblebees freighted with pollen
buzz by again, again,
fixed by her calyx tilt,
tasting her multicolored tongue.
They're drunk, forgetful,
as if no winter ever were.
As if soft swellings such as hers
will sway forever in whatever wind.

AT THE TEMPLE OF APHRODITE

Aphrodisias, Turkey, September

The fragrance of white clover
no bigger than the new toes of babies
intoxicates an entire valley.
Bees stumble, butterflies whirl, finches dance.

Dionysus laughs from the stone
shoulders of satyrs
wrapped in garlands of plums.
A marble mountain, crowned ten million

summers' white, shines over this city built
by a freed slave to his love of Love.
Two thousand years have flowered before we
see her smooth, carved blossoms

garlanding the ground at Aphrodite's
imposing entrance, where pious
muezzins call from two directions
for midday prayer. We pray . . .

to the fragrance of loved stone,
tousled heads and limbs and torsos,
whole epics frozen in marble against cerulean sky.
We are all slaves in this Temple where love began

at a nearby spring and ends in sweetness
bubbling from cubes of sugar breathing in clear tea
near a plate of olives and ripe tomatoes
set before you, my peerless Aphrodite.

SWIMMING IN THE SEA OF TIME

The book in my hands is by Wallace Stegner,
about friendship it turns out, and my mind
wanders back over forty-six years
to when we too were just married,
a basement apartment, the first baby
in the crib in our closet, a new friend
across the hall in the janitor's closet.

Soon enough we visited another friend,
witnessed his marriage, today a doctor any of us
would want, avuncular and truth-telling,
visited him again, his house in the mountains.

The doctor sent me *Crossing to Safety* last spring,
insisted we read it, and so today,
Saturday at dawn, before the celebration
of other friends' fortieth anniversary,
who drew us to New York,
my wife driving here with her friend
since summer camp, now my friend too,

I stumble around my sister-in-law's
apartment, drunk on coffee,
swimming in a sea of time,
window open, air humid and gray,

breeze swaddling me,
garbage trucks groaning below,
the view a universe of rooftops.

NEW NEW MEXICO WOMAN

for granddaughter Olivia, one day old

Already this question answered:
Can you breathe in light so sharp it makes gods
shudder, pulls artists to their knees?

My northern eyes burn
from the bright light of your birth.
When I visit, I'll bring my watery hand.
When we touch, you will not forget
the odd warp of my middle nail,
the raised blue veins like seagrass
under water.

And I will bring this vow.
We will go together among
my lakes, your hills.
These will not be stories that we tell
but waters that we swim
and air we breathe.

Your eyes will grow as sharp as
all the artists where you live, who,
shocked by the beauty of the world,
fight for it, peacefully, all their lives.

And you will leap in my sweet waters
like a seal sounding in the waves,
rising open-eyed and laughing
from the buoyancy that birthed us all.

YOU KNOW WHAT I KNOW

for Henno

I met you four days old,
your skull soft as petals,
brows flowing over your cheeks
like standing waves,
eyes sealed against
a blizzard's light.

In two days as we walked
in gathering snow,
you feasted on our air,
our daughter's milk,
your thumb.

I held you six days old
to say goodbye,
rocked you back and forth
within our breath.

You winked at me—
one eye blue and black at once,
part fish, part bird—
and raised an impish smile
at the corner of your mouth.

I saw my father,
his eightieth birthday,
pacing back and forth
framing the stories
he would tell to friends
who waited, wondering
what he knew.

At my grave, you'll look up
toward rustling leaves in winter,
a busy, hammering woodpecker,
the two-note whistling love call
of the chickadee I will teach you.
Again, your lip will rise at the corner.
Again one eye winks at the sun.

You know what I know.
There is no death.

THE POET VISITS HIS SON, A CONCERT PROMOTER, AND ATTENDS A MICHAEL FRANTI CONCERT

It is quiet I long for, that calls forth ecstasy
the way a river calls forth its mouth,
the stillness of shimmer in dry leaves,
the vivid fall colors of dreams,
the fascination of the grave.

Yet here, under booming speakers tall as buildings,
fifteen hundred of us rise up on our toes,
men old as me, and children spinning,
all waving and clapping our palms,
giving our bodies away to this gentle man
and his guitarist with hair like a goat,
the African drummer with the voice of a bird,
Franti's dreadlocked head and open heart,
his body's music a holy poem.

What a bargain at thirty-five dollars a ticket,
my son behind the scenes the way parents sweat
and worry profit and loss behind the scenes.

Tonight a line of glowing strangers thanks my son.
Michael thanks him.
I too shake his hand.

DANCING AT WINTER SOLSTICE

We live where city lights make time obscure.
We do not know how bright day is,
how dark night.

One must travel half a world
for mountain priests
to catch the sun and bring it back again.
They know that if sun goes, hope goes.

Stars spin stories of our birth
and sing us holy songs,
but there's too much light between
to feed the heart.
The moon laughs or cries,
who really knows?

Last night we danced and drank so late
the sun, stirred from its grave,
burned off the frost that coats our hearts.
I reached to touch the hairs above your wrist.
They blossomed at your thigh.
Stars rose and fell and rose again
in the fire of your eyes.

WILD SWANS NEAR GLADSTONE

A pair of swans lingers in the bay
opposite the freeway in upper Michigan in summer.
"Mated for life," I point out to my wife.
"Mute swans," she says, not looking,
"no need to talk." I note the graceful mute life,
she driving her quiet Prius, me a quiet guest.
When her eyes, weary, reluctantly offer me
the wheel, it is like relinquishing a broken
sword into tall grass after a day of battle.
Now my turn to drive, and my mind wanders
over the pair of elegant swans seen every time
we pass the curve of the bay together, or alone.

BEFORE THE GRANDCHILDREN ARRIVE

This is a morning for chores, reading, poems.
Because tomorrow, early, the bedroom door
will creak open with the sun
and the word "Grandpa" flood in like
Sergeant Pepper's Lonely Hearts Club Band,
marching me up off the sheets and back
into the beauty of the world,
like a young Lewis or Clark
or exhausted Magellan,
or the billion other grandparents
sensing again the web of the world,
hearing again its spinning song.

WATCHING GUS DRAW

Dawn on a still day, I am reading
Kim Stafford's *Early Morning*,
a memoir of his quiet poet father,
when Gus comes down. We brush fingertips,
enough touch for this time of day, and he sits,
his nine-year-old body fuzzy with sleep.
After a while, he has decided to draw,
for he arrives at the table next to me with
instruction books and colored pencils.

As I slowly conclude the chapter
"Millions of Intricate Moves,"
Gus sits cross-legged on a wicker chaise
inspecting the open art book,
then executing its strokes,
sunlight tousling his red-gold hair.

So this is how this physical boy spends
an early morning,
before the bicycle of his body propels him
off at great speed through the humming day.

I watch him from the warmth
of Stafford's open hand,
raising my eyebrow perhaps a quarter inch

as Gus retrieves a dropped pencil
and discovers the spider's web beneath
the chaise, and the corpse of a wasp.

END OF SUMMER

Fog hangs over the Straits. Iron ore
freighters call out, dragging their
heavy bellies toward distant kilns.

I build a fire from birch split that afternoon,
push charred ends toward the center.
My hands darken with ash.

I pick two poems to read at dinner
from the manuscript of a friend,
dead now, with us here.

Above me, a son sings in the shower.
From the kitchen, lemon and garlic.
Down the stairs, a daughter's perfume.

A MIRROR IN ROME

In the mirror you say
you see a worn woman.
And that you've earned
your worry lines and evidence
of gravity's steady pull
and enough money
to erase them both with
a modern sculptor's scalpel
if you choose.

But when I look at you
from behind my trifocals
over a white blizzard of beard
that hides the cave of
my few words,

I see you standing as only
you have stood before me,
your callipygian tilt the model
for that famous sculpture
now in Naples,
your skin radiant as fox fire
from the memory
of four sublime babies
now wandering like Aeneas
this protean earth,
no sculpture more beautiful than this.

When I am laid
to rest
next to you
in the glaciated soils
of Minneapolis or Mackinac,
we will have little to say
to each other over that distance
wide as a kitchen table,
the stories of our lives written
in what we did together,
not the silences between.

You'll finally sleep easily
on your side of the plot,
all ash and wind and water,
a line of polished wisdom on your self-effacing stone.
On my side the heavy, messy snore
of fungus and tree roots and moles' nests,
a granite animal howling and scratching above me.

Once before that, I'd love
to take the woman in the mirror to Rome.
To sit at a sidewalk café sipping
cappuccino and grappa
in the roar of Roman traffic
through the lovely rubble of time,
the Rome Piranesi etched,
the Rome Antonioni filmed,

the Rome Shelley praised in poems
"like flame transformed to marble."

And hold, for only the moment you
will allow me before shyly pulling away
both your hands in both of mine,

and thank you, from the boy I was before
to the man bent before you,
for all the life blossoming around me,
storied, sunlit, timelessly beautiful.

HERE IS MY PROMISE TO YOU, OR
MARCO POLO LEAVES THE KITCHEN
FOR THE PROVINCES

Every morning battered knees and ankles allow
I will rise in the dark and empty the dishwasher,
quietly setting away plates and spoons
so we begin the trek of day uncluttered.

Every morning I will read the dispatches from
the outer world and leave those facts arranged
on the kitchen table for you to plot
our escape well-armed.

Every morning when the sun breaks
over the neighbor's ragged shingles
I will worry with you about the children and the babies,
how they are faring on the long trail we have blazed.

And every morning when black coffee charges me
like Marco Polo onto the Silk Road toward distant
China I will set out to write the wonders
my wanderings discover.

So that when you appear in the doorway,
companion still swaddled in the royal blue of night,
my body will swiftly clear the tent
for you to rule as you do so well in silver light.

Between sunrise and sunset I will be away
from your mysteries into the extremities of mine.

Otherwise you can count on me to execute my tasks.
Just as, after dark, I am certain to settle under the sheets
of evening like a blowing, hibernating bear.
Wake me if need be, but know I will be
useless as you address the riddles
of the day, the calamities of night.

But let me tell you as the sun sets what I learned
today. Ahead lies a golden city. Below its parapets
white horses graze. Inside waits a robe embroidered
with a million golden threads.
It lies in the hollow of the valley
over the mountains of your shoulders.
There an emperor, barely a child, slew all his slaves
to banish death. And left behind for us a monument
in the earth, filled, it is said, with rivers of mercury,
stars of diamonds, crossbows set to foil intruders.

Take my hand and let us brave that sight.
Together we have once again survived
the murderous robberies of the night.

WHEN I AM EIGHTY

When I am eighty
I am going to throw a big party
for myself.

When I am eighty
I am going to dress up
in white pants
and a white shirt
with black suspenders
and let a white horse
eat out of my hand.

When I am eighty
I am going to get up
at three in the morning
and pace and think
in the quiet.

When I am eighty
I am going to tell story after story
and laugh and laugh
and think all my ideas
are good ones.

When I am eighty
I'm going to be mad as hell
if you don't do it my way.

When I am eighty
I am going to send grandchildren
on treks along backcountry streams
and go home and read the newspaper.
Because I will know it is younger people
who now must find the lost.
But without me
no one would have any
good stories to tell.

When I am eighty
I will hold the fine silk goblet
of my wife in both my hands.
That will be all the life
I can handle.

EPILOGUE

WEDDING POEM

Marriage is attached
to the center of earth.
Its weight is incalculable.

Before,
it swirls around you
like a gas,
like a collection of stuffed animals,
like a forest fire.

But after the ritual
under the arbor,
the sharing of tea,
the grin of the justice,
the white train floating like a glacier
down the red aisle,
the looping of rings,
the moon dance . . .

it attaches to the feet.
It weighs them down
and supports them
at once.

It is gravity,
which limits us totally,
which makes all life possible.

Acknowledgments

Many of these poems originally appeared in the following periodicals:
Amaranth Review, Art Word Quarterly, Askew, Aurorean, Black Buzzard Review, Borealis, Chronicle Alternative, Concrete Wolf, Echoes, Free Verse, Goodrichie, Ha!, Journal of Family Life, Lilliput Review, Minnesota Monthly, Mojo Risin', North American Review, North Central Review, Ophelia's Pale Lilies, Poetry Calendar 1999, Poets On: Refusing, Rag Mag, Recycled Quarterly, Rosebud, Sidewalks, Urthona (UK), *Verse Wisconsin, Water-Stone, Whistling Shade.*

The following poems were published in anthologies: "Backscratch Boy" in *Essential Love: Poems about Mothers and Fathers, Daughters and Sons*, ed. Ginny Lowe Connors, and in *The Well-Versed Parent: Poetic Prescriptions for Parenthood*, ed. Jane E. Hunter, MD; "My Wife Sleeping beside Me" in *Proposing on the Brooklyn Bridge: Poems on Marriage*, ed. Ginny Lowe Connors; "An Engineering Problem" in *Poets On: 20th Anniversary Reprise*, ed. Ruth Daigon; "When You Are Ready, Climb" and "The Morning of the Wedding" in *My Heart's First Steps*; "To Make a Baby" in *Family Matters: Poems of Our Families*; "A Mirror in Rome" in *25 Minnesota Poets/2014.*

Thanks to the editors for permission to reprint.
Special gratitude to the Anderson Center for residencies which allowed me to organize and revise this manuscript. And to poet, teacher, editor, and friend Thomas R. Smith, always the first reader of my poems.

JAMES P. LENFESTEY is a former college English instructor, alternative school administrator, marketing communications consultant, and editorial writer for the *Minneapolis Star Tribune*, where he won several Page One awards for excellence. Since 2000, he has published a memoir, *Seeking the Cave: A Pilgrimage to Cold Mountain*, a collection of personal essays and five collections of poems. He edited two poetry anthologies and coedited *Robert Bly in This World*. As a journalist, he has covered education, energy policy, and climate science. He lives in Minneapolis with his wife of fifty years. They have four children and eight grandchildren.

milkweed
editions

Founded as a nonprofit organization in 1980, Milkweed
Editions is an independent publisher. Our mission is to
identify, nurture and publish transformative literature,
and build an engaged community around it.

milkweed.org

Interior design by Mary Austin Speaker
Typeset in Caslon
by Mary Austin Speaker

Adobe Caslon Pro was created by Carol Twombly for
Adobe Systems in 1990. Her design was inspired by the
family of typefaces cut by the celebrated engraver
William Caslon I, whose family foundry served
England with clean, elegant type from the early
Enlightenment through the turn of the
twentieth century.